I0532978

HAUNTED ARIZONA

ARIZONA

DEADLY GRAVEYARDS

HAUNTED ARIZONA

DEADLY GRAVEYARDS

13 Fatal Cemetery Stories

JETHRO BLANCH

Haunted Arizona Deadly Graveyards: 13 Fatal Cemetery Stories
September 2024

Published by Paranormal Playground
Phoenix, Arizona

Copyright © 2024 by Jethro Blanch
All rights reserved

Photography by Jethro Blanch

ISBN 979-8-89542-000-3
LCCN 2024916241

Publisher's Cataloging-in-Publication data
Names: Blanch, Jethro, author.
Title: Haunted Arizona Deadly Graveyards: 13 Fatal Cemetery Stories / Jethro Blanch.
Description: Includes bibliographical references. | Phoenix, AZ: Paranormal Playground, 2024.
Identifiers: LCCN: 2024916241 | ISBN: 979-8-89542-000-3 (paperback) | 979-8-89542-001-0 (hardcover) | 979-8-89542-002-7 (ebook) | 979-8-89542-003-4 (audiobook)
Subjects: LCSH Ghosts--Arizona. | Haunted places--Arizona. | Cemeteries--Arizona. | Arizona--History. | BISAC BODY, MIND & SPIRIT / Supernatural (incl. Ghosts) | TRAVEL / Special Interest / Haunted & Unexplained | HISTORY / United States / State & Local / Southwest (AZ, NM, OK, TX)
Classification: LCC BF1472.U6 B53 2024 | DDC 133.109791--dc23

No part of this book may be reproduced in any form, without prior written permission from the author or publisher, except in the case of brief quotations embodied in critical articles or reviews.

Manufactured in the United States of America

Contents

Introduction

Arizona's sprawling desert landscape and historic towns are often celebrated for their natural beauty and vibrant history. However, beneath the sun-drenched surface lies a darker, more enigmatic side of the state's past. *Haunted Arizona Deadly Graveyards* dives into the chilling tales of those whose lives ended amid the eerie silence of Arizona's cemeteries. This book goes beyond simply recounting tragic endings—it is an exploration of the haunting mysteries and lingering spirits that continue to fascinate the imaginations of paranormal enthusiasts and haunted historians alike.

Each chapter in this collection unveils a story of profound despair and the final, desperate acts committed in some of Arizona's most historic resting places. From the heart-wrenching farewell of John Moore in Greenwood Cemetery to the mysterious demise of Jim Chafin in Resthaven Park, these accounts paint a vivid picture of human sorrow intertwined with supernatural intrigue.

These cemeteries, now silent witnesses to these tragic events, carry an air of melancholy and mystery. They are places where history and the paranormal intersect, offering glimpses into the lives of those who, in their moments of deepest despair, sought solace among the dead. The stories are meticulously researched, drawing from historical records, newspaper articles, and eyewitness accounts to bring to life the final moments of these individuals.

For those with a passion for the paranormal, these cemeteries are more than mere burial grounds; they are potential hot-spots for ghostly activity. The echoes of the past resonate through these hallowed grounds, and many believe that the spirits of those who met their end in such tragic ways linger, their stories etched into the very fabric of these sacred places.

Introduction

As you turn the pages of *Haunted Arizona Deadly Graveyards*, you will journey through tales of love, loss, and the inexplicable draw of the afterlife. Whether you are a seasoned ghost hunter or a curious reader, these stories will captivate your imagination and perhaps, just perhaps, make you wonder about the restless souls that might still wander Arizona's cemeteries.

Prepare yourself for an unforgettable exploration into the depths of despair and the supernatural, where each chapter uncovers a new layer of Arizona's haunted history, leaving you with more questions than answers and a sense of awe at the enduring mystery of life and death.

CHAPTER 1

REBECA MOORE
1848 — 1920

VED, LIVED & DIED FOR
HER FELLOWMAN.

John Moore, Phoenix

Greenwood Cemetery, April 25, 1924

John Moore was a man who had witnessed the transformation of Arizona from a rugged frontier to a budding state. Born in 1850, he arrived in Phoenix in 1867, seeking fortune and a new beginning. For decades, he worked hard, running a blacksmith shop near Five Points and later working for the Water Users Association. Despite his contributions, life had not been kind to John in his later years.

By the year 1924, at the age of 74, John found himself facing insurmountable financial difficulties. He had been living at the Union Hotel for eight months, unable to escape the despair that had gripped him. His wife Rebeca had passed away, leaving a void that only grew larger with each passing day. Alone and despondent, John felt his options dwindling.

On a warm April afternoon, John made his way to Greenwood Cemetery. The superintendent of the cemetery, having seen the elderly man walk through the gate shortly after 3:00 p.m., noted how John headed towards the southwest corner where his wife's grave was located. The family plot was a solemn reminder of the life he once had, and the love he had lost.

Greenwood Cemetery, section 22

As he approached the monument bearing his wife's name, John leaned against it, seeking comfort one last time. He had brought with him a .25 caliber pistol. With a heavy heart and a clear resolve, he pressed the gun to his right temple and pulled the trigger.

The sound of the shot echoed through the cemetery, drawing the attention of two employees who quickly informed the superintendent. They hurried to the scene and discovered John lying in a pool of blood, his head resting against his wife's grave.

Despite their attempts to save him, John was later transported to St. Joseph's Hospital, where he was pronounced dead.

Rebeca Moore's gravesite, section 22

Back at the Union Hotel, a search of John Moore's room revealed a small handbag containing a farewell note addressed to Thomas McCubbin, the hotel proprietor. The note, written with a steady hand, read:

Dear Mack,

I leave to you all I have to pay for my room. I think you will find enough. Dispose of everything that I have left and pay the room rent and I think there will be enough left to pay Mr. Reynolds $10.00. Thank you and the lady of the house for your kindness. They will not give me a chance to live and work, so goodbye. I have done my best trying. I am going on a long trip. I am not crazy, nor a coward, but what is the use? I have done my duty, so goodbye.

J. W. Moore

Inside his pocket, they found an envelope with the words, "Please let me rest here," scrawled on it. His belongings were few; a roll of bedding, two suitcases, and the small handbag. John's only known relatives were a daughter, Lydia, residing in Redding, California, and a sister in Oregon. Notification of John's death was promptly sent to them by the McLellan Undertaking Company, who had taken charge of his body.

John Moore's life, marked by perseverance and toil, ended in the quiet corner of Greenwood Cemetery. Though his final moments were filled with sorrow, he found solace in reuniting, in spirit, with his beloved wife.

Greenwood Memorial Park was established in 1906 by the Free and Accepted Masons. In 1947, the Shumway family founded Memory Lawn Memorial Park just to the west. Though originally separated by a fence, Memory Lawn later expanded to include a mortuary, mausoleum, and chapel. The two cemeteries merged in 1989, becoming Greenwood Memory Lawn Cemetery.

Its grounds were intended as a place of peace and remembrance. Yet over the years, it has become known for more than just its history and headstones. Multiple deaths have occurred within the cemetery gates, and visitors often report unsettling experiences—cold chills on hot days, fleeting shadows drifting between graves, and faint whispers that seem to rise from nowhere. Among the cemetery's many rumored spirits, some believe John Moore still lingers near Rebeca's grave—forever bound to the woman he loved, silently keeping watch at the very spot where he drew his final breath.

The graves of John and Rebeca Moore are located at Greenwood Memory Lawn Cemetery in Phoenix. John was interred in section 25, while Rebeca's gravesite, where John took his life, is in section 22.

Rebeca Moore's tombstone, 33.453331, -112.111976

Greenwood Cemetery aerial view, 2024

Greenwood Memory Lawn Mortuary & Cemetery
2300 W. Van Buren St., Phoenix, AZ 85009

Alan Moore: Phoenix

James Mitchell, Phoenix

Forest Lawn Cemetery, August 16, 1926

James Mitchell had always been a man of quiet strength and determination. At 27, he had already faced more hardship than many people experience in a lifetime. But nothing had prepared him for the loss of his beloved wife. She had recently passed away, leaving a void in his heart that he could not fill. Despondent and unable to cope with his grief, James decided that he could no longer continue without her.

On a hot summer day in 1926, James returned home to Phoenix from a trip to Los Angeles. He had arrived carrying a heavy burden and a plan that he had meticulously crafted. The caretaker of Forest Lawn Cemetery, J. M. Hendricks, had noticed James visiting his wife's grave several times over the last few days. He had seen him place artificial flowers on her grave one morning and returned with a large bouquet of cut flowers the following day.

As the sun climbed higher in the sky, James placed the fresh flowers on his wife's grave, his heart aching with every motion. He stood there for a long time, lost in his memories and sorrow. Then, with a heavy heart and trembling hands, he took out a gun he had purchased for $10.50, aimed it at his head, and pulled the trigger.

Forest Lawn section of Greenwood Cemetery, 33.451986, -112.109288

11

The sound of the shot echoed through the cemetery. Caretaker Hendricks, who was nearby, heard the shot and went to investigate. He found nothing at first but later discovered James' lifeless body sprawled across his wife's grave. The tragedy had taken place around noon, and Hendricks found the body at about 2:00 p.m. He immediately notified the authorities.

Coroner Clarence E. Ice arrived on the scene, accompanied by County Physician Harry J. Felch. Upon examining James' body, they found a note addressed to his sister living on the West Coast. The note was terse, stating that since his wife's death, he had lost all interest in life and had no desire to continue. It included instructions for his automobile to be given to his sister, though the car was not found in Phoenix, leading authorities to believe it had been left in Los Angeles.

James had carefully prepared for this final act. The note revealed he had about $58.00 with him, of which $10.50 had been spent on the gun, $2.00 on flowers for his wife's grave, and the remaining amount was found in a money order with some silver coins.

James' body was taken to the parlors of Yarwood and Hockery Undertaking Company, where it awaited word from his relatives. Coroner Ice declared the death a suicide and confirmed that no inquest would be necessary.

James Mitchell's life ended in the place that held the remains of his greatest love, a bitter testament to the depth of his grief and the strength of his devotion.

Greenwood Memorial Park was established in 1906, followed by the creation of Memory Lawn Memorial Park just to the west in 1947. Over time, Forest Lawn Cemetery was also absorbed into the expanding grounds. In 1989, the once-separate cemeteries were unified under one name: Greenwood Memory Lawn Cemetery.

James Mitchell's story echoes that of John Moore, another grieving widower whose sorrow brought him to the same cemetery gates. Stories like theirs fuel the belief that Greenwood is more than just a resting place. Over the years, multiple deaths have occurred within its borders, and countless visitors have reported unsettling sensations—sudden chills, drifting shadows, and whispers that rise from the silence. Among the spirits said to haunt the grounds, some believe James Mitchell still walks among the graves, just like John Moore before him—bound by love, sorrow, and a promise that death could not break.

The Mitchells' final resting place is in the old Forest Lawn section of what is now Greenwood Memory Lawn Cemetery in Phoenix. James was laid to rest in Section FL-31, while his wife's gravesite, where James ended his life, is in section FL-30.

Forest Lawn Cemetery aerial view, 2024

Greenwood Memory Lawn Mortuary & Cemetery
2300 W. Van Buren St., Phoenix, AZ 85009

CHAPTER 3

Eulogio Molina, Nogales

Nogales Cemetery, June 7, 1930

In the early summer of 1930, the border town of Nogales was abuzz with the tragic news of Eulogio Molina's passing. Born in 1850, Eulogio had lived through the tumultuous times of the American Southwest, witnessing the transformation of Arizona from a rough territory to a settled state. His life was marked by resilience and steadfast composure, yet it was his death that garnered the most attention.

Eulogio was employed by the city of Nogales as a gravedigger for the city cemetery, a job that embodied his devoted and unassuming character. For years, he tended to the final resting places of the town's deceased, ensuring that each grave was dug with care and respect. His work was largely unnoticed, a quiet service to the community he had called home for so many years.

Nogales Cemetery, 2024

On June 7, 1930, as the sun cast its warm glow over Nogales, Eulogio was performing his usual duties in the cemetery. In a tragic twist of fate, he fell over dead and into a grave he was filling. The suddenness of his death sent shockwaves through the town, leaving residents in mourning for the man who had faithfully served them.

Eulogio Molina was laid to rest in the very cemetery where he had worked, his final resting place unmarked, yet his presence deeply felt. Though no monument commemorates his life, his legacy endures in the hearts of the people of Nogales.

Nogales City Cemetery was officially established in 1905 on a hill overlooking the future site of U.S. Army Camp Little, which would be founded five years later. However, several burials had already taken place there prior to its formal designation. Today, all plots in the public section have been sold. Known as a cross-border cultural melting pot, the cemetery reflects the rich and complex heritage of the Nogales community.

Some believe the grounds are haunted, and local legend holds that Eulogio Molina, the longtime gravedigger, still watches over the cemetery—even in death. There are even tales of a phantom vehicle seen racing along the highway from Nogales to Tucson, vanishing without a trace.

Nogales Cemetery aerial view, 1975

Nogales Cemetery gate

Nogales Cemetery
W. Western Ave., Nogales, AZ 85621

CHAPTER 4

MARGARET SANDERS
HOLMES

MAY 19, 1887
FEB. 6, 1952

Julian Holmes, Phoenix

Greenwood Cemetery, February 23, 1954

In February 1954, the city of Phoenix was struck by the tragic story of Julian Holmes, a prominent real estate agent. Julian, who had been a resident of Phoenix since 1913, was deeply mourning the loss of his wife who had passed away two years prior. Julian was well-known in the community, having been a founder of the Phoenix Country Club and a member of the Arizona Club.

Tragically, Julian's story concluded with his death on his wife Margaret's grave in Greenwood Cemetery, having taken his own life with a Colt six-shooter. In a touching final gesture, he had carefully placed six small bunches of orange and white flowers on her grave before ending his life. The last person to see him alive, Pedro Lastra, a cemetery employee, saw Julian walk towards the grave but lost sight of him before hearing the fatal shot.

Greenwood Cemetery, section 13

Despite being in poor health, Julian's co-workers at A.D. McClain Realty Company were shocked by his death, as he had called them just 30 minutes earlier, indicating he was on his way to work.

William Edwin Julian Holmes Sr. was born on November 24, 1886, in Gibson County, Tennessee, to Dr. William Newton Holmes and Margaret Learned Holmes. Raised in a family of medical professionals and scholars, Julian developed a strong work ethic and a commitment to community service. His World War I registration card reflected a man ready to serve his country.

The story of Julian and Margaret Holmes is one of dedication, resilience, and service. Their lives, intertwined with the history of Arizona, serve as a reminder of the lasting impact individuals can have on their communities. As Phoenix continues to grow and evolve, the memory of the Holmes family remains a cornerstone of its rich history.

Since its opening in 1906, a heavy cloud has lingered over Greenwood Cemetery—a presence that many believe is more than just the weight of time. Whispers of the paranormal have long surrounded these grounds, where countless visitors have reported unexplained chills, fleeting shadows, and a sense of being watched. Among the spirits said to roam, it's believed that Julian Holmes still sits quietly beside his wife's grave—just as John Moore and James Mitchell are said to do. Their lingering presence is a haunting reminder that not every soul laid to rest here has truly moved on.

The graves of Julian and Margaret Holmes are located in section 13 at Greenwood Memory Lawn Cemetery in Phoenix.

Margaret Holmes' tombstone, 33.454390, -112.109849

Greenwood Cemetery aerial view, 1954

Greenwood Cemetery aerial view, 2024

Greenwood Memory Lawn Mortuary & Cemetery
719 N. 27th Ave., Phoenix, AZ 85009

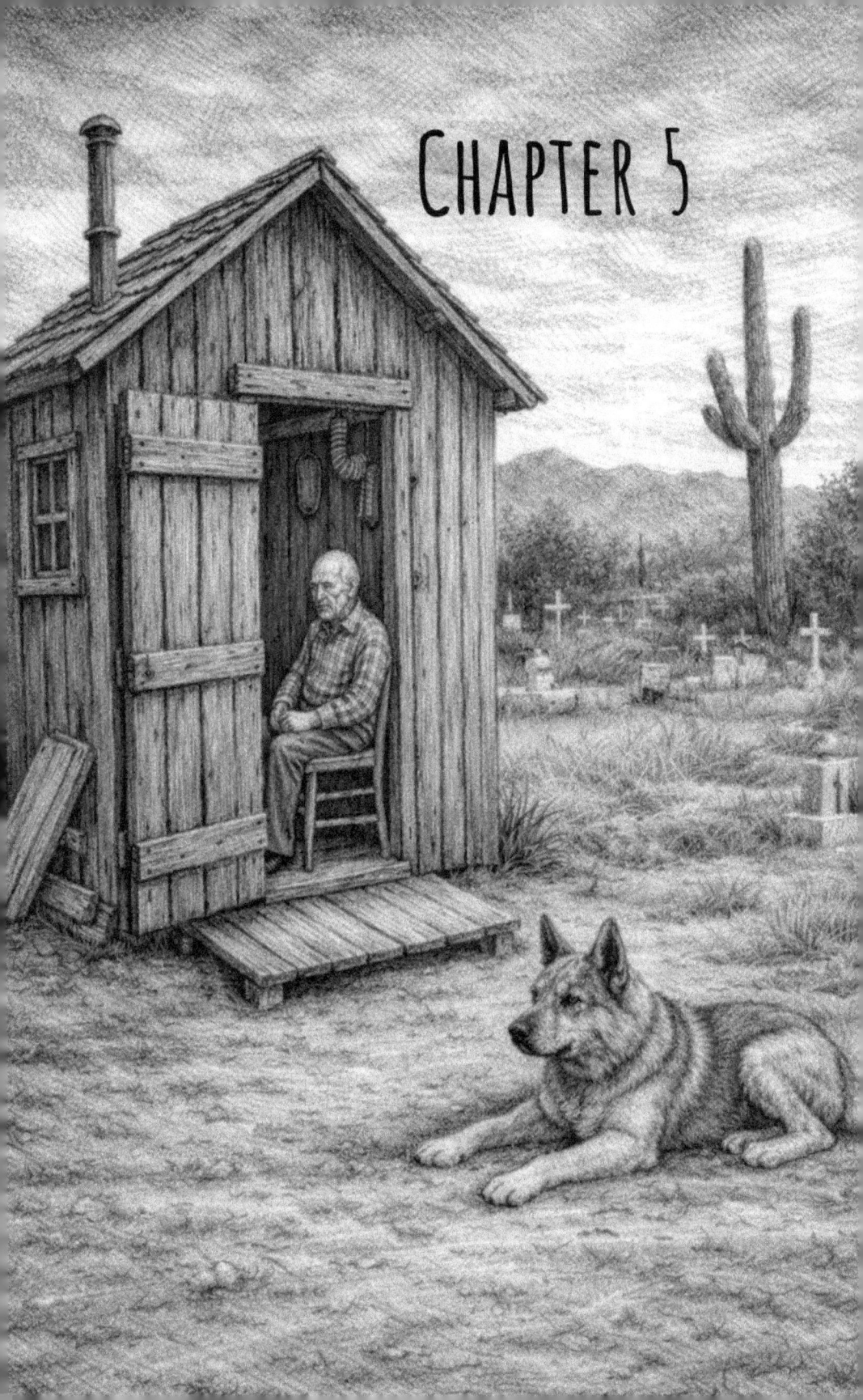

CHAPTER 5

Andres Serna, Superior

Fairview Cemetery, June 16, 1956

Andres Serna lived a remarkable life that spanned a century of profound change and development in Arizona. Throughout his years, Andres observed the transformation of the Arizona Territory into a modern state. Resilient and enduring, he left an unforgettable mark on his community in Superior.

Born on June 7, 1856, Andres lived through the Indian Wars, witnessed the arrival of the railroad, and saw the dawn of Arizona's statehood, adapting to each new era with grace and determination. In 1956, on a hot summer day in mid-June, Andres' life came to a quiet end.

H. M. Smith, the owner of a funeral home, found the old man dead in his shack next to Fairview Cemetery, during a routine visit to deliver his pension check. The centenarian had worked as a gravedigger at the cemetery from 1935 up until just a few years prior when old age forced him to retire. Andres lived alone with his dog, chickens, a cat, and a burro. After his passing, his loyal canine kept a lonely vigil in the shack while the other animals wandered off.

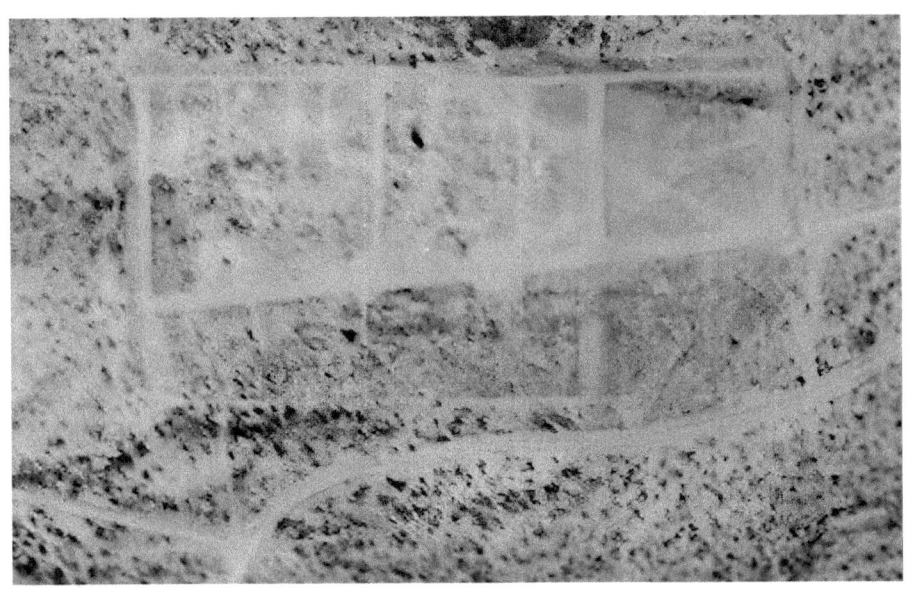

Fairview Cemetery aerial view, 1945

Andres Serna's century-spanning life is a testament to the enduring spirit of those who settled and shaped the American Southwest. His story, filled with whispered mysteries and community reverence, continues to inspire and intrigue. As the town of Superior grows and changes, the memory of Andres serves as a gentle reminder of its rich and storied past.

In 1916, Fairview Cemetery became the primary burial ground for Superior, taking the place of the earlier Historic Pinal Cemetery. The old cemetery had once served the bustling mining town of Pinal—a community that vanished after the Silver King Mine shut down in 1888. Today, all that remains of Pinal are scattered gravestones and the faint echoes of a town long forgotten.

In more recent years, Fairview Cemetery has become the subject of paranormal curiosity. A handful of untimely deaths have occurred within its gates, and several locals have reported eerie happenings—mysterious lights, distant whispers, and the sensation of unseen eyes watching from the shadows. Some say the spirit of Andres Serna, accompanied by the ghost of his faithful dog, still roams the cemetery grounds, keeping watch over the resting place he once tended with such care.

Andres Serna was buried in the same cemetery where he worked for so many years. His grave is located in section 13 at Fairview Cemetery in Superior.

Fairview Cemetery, section 13

Andres Serna's grave marker, 33.280293, -111.113466

Fairview Cemetery main gate, 2012

Fairview Cemetery
300 W. Sunset Dr., Superior, AZ 85173

CHAPTER 6

Rob Gastelum, Tucson

Evergreen Cemetery, February 7, 1957

Robert S. Gastelum was known for his quiet demeanor and dedication to his family. He was born on October 10, 1932, in Tucson, to Frank and Mary Gastelum. As Rob reached adulthood, he served his country in the U.S. Navy, a role that brought him both pride and a heavy burden.

Despite his service and the support of his family, Rob struggled with severe depression. His mental health battles were a constant companion, often overshadowing the achievements and joys of his young life. By the time he reached 24, the weight of his struggles had become unbearable.

On the morning of February 7, 1957, Rob made his way to Evergreen Cemetery in Tucson. The peaceful surroundings of the cemetery, with its rows of gravestones and quiet paths, became the backdrop for his final moments. In a state of deep despair, Rob shot himself in the head with a small caliber pistol. When he was found, he was still alive, slumped over a marble slab. He was rushed to the hospital, but the injuries were too severe, and he was pronounced deceased.

Evergreen Cemetery from West Fort Lowell Road, 2024

Rob was laid to rest in Holy Hope Cemetery, which sits right next to Evergreen. His grave stands as a silent testament to his brief and tumultuous life. The death of Robert Gastelum serves as a tragic reminder of the hidden battles many face and the importance of mental health support. His story is one of service, struggle, and a community's enduring sorrow, underscoring the need for compassion and understanding in the face of such profound personal pain.

Evergreen and Holy Hope Cemeteries, both established in 1907, serve as the final resting places for many of Tucson's earliest and most notable residents.

Some visitors have reported eerie experiences — most often, the unmistakable sound of children running and laughing, echoing through the cemetery when no one is in sight. One woman even claimed that something unseen yanked her hair, though she was alone at the time. Perhaps it was the mischievous spirit of young Rob Gastelum, still playing pranks from beyond the grave.

The gravesite of Robert Gastelum is located in section 11N at Greenwood Holy Hope Cemetery in Tucson.

Evergreen & Holy Hope Cemeteries aerial view, 1958

Robert Gastelum's gravesite at Holy Hope Cemetery, 2024

Robert Gastelum's grave marker, 32.269361, -110.980528

Holy Hope Cemetery Oracle Road entrance, 2024

Holy Hope Cemetery
3555 N. Oracle Rd., Tucson, AZ 85705

Evergreen Cemetery Miracle Mile entrance, 2024

Evergreen Mortuary, Cemetery, and Crematory
3015 N. Oracle Rd., Tucson, AZ 85705

Chapter 7

Ward Bradish, Tucson

Evergreen Cemetery, October 7, 1964

On a crisp November morning in 1964, Tucson police faced a grim discovery near Evergreen Cemetery. A decomposed body had been found by a 28-year-old resident, while he was clearing high weeds near the Miracle Mile entrance of the cemetery.

Evergreen Cemetery Miracle Mile entrance, 2024

The body was later identified as 59-year-old Ward Orin Bradish Sr., who had been missing since October 7, after being reported by a concerned neighbor. The identification process was complex. It was the discovery of his name written in laundry ink on his clothing that provided the crucial clue. This was further corroborated by an acquaintance who recognized the clothing as what Ward had been wearing when last seen.

The cause of death, as determined by Dr. Louis Hirsch, the coroner's pathologist, was due to natural causes, likely exacerbated by exposure. Ward's untimely demise left the community in shock and raised many questions about how he ended up in such a state.

Ward lived nearby on West Laguna Street, a quiet neighborhood that was rattled by the news. His neighbors described him as a solitary man who kept mostly to himself. Despite his reserved nature, Ward's sudden disappearance and subsequent death created a solemn mood among the residents.

Frank Borquez, who stumbled upon Ward's body, was deeply affected by the find. His routine task of clearing weeds had turned into a harrowing experience. The incident left a lasting impact on Borquez, who struggled to shake off the eerie memory of that day.

The story of Ward Bradish is a sentimental reminder of the fragility of life and the mysteries that often surround us. As the community of Tucson slowly came to terms with the loss, Ward's tale became a part of the local lore, a story of a man who, in death, brought a community together in their collective grief and curiosity.

Evergreen and Pima County Cemeteries were both established in 1907. Over time, the remains of many early pioneers from remote ranches and homesteads were relocated and reburied within Evergreen's expanding grounds.

Visitors to the cemetery often speak of chilling encounters, including the unmistakable sound of children laughing and playing when no one is there. Some claim to have been touched by unseen hands. A handful of deaths have occurred within the cemetery itself, including that of Robert Gastelum. Some wonder if he and Ward Bradish still wander the grounds, their spirits lingering among the graves.

Ward Bradish was buried in the Pima County Cemetery, located in the northwest corner of Evergreen Cemetery.

Ward Bradish's gravesite, 2024

Ward Bradish's grave marker

Pima County Cemetery, 32.265679, -110.984479

Pima County Cemetery aerial view, 2024

Evergreen & Pima County Cemeteries aerial view, 1966

Evergreen Mortuary, Cemetery, and Crematory
3015 N. Oracle Rd., Tucson, AZ 85705

Chapter 8

Joyce Gutierrez, Scottsdale

Green Acres Cemetery, July 6, 1977

Rudolph V. "Rudy" Gutierrez was a vibrant young man, known for his dedication and hard work. He found employment with Blue Cross & Blue Shield and built a promising future for himself. Rudy later met and married Joyce Marian Boudette in Ohio. The couple eventually moved from Dayton and settled in the Phoenix area, eager to start their life together.

However, beneath the couple's seemingly perfect life, Rudy struggled with deep-seated personal issues and their lives became intertwined in a tale of love and tragedy. On December 9, 1975, at the young age of 20, Rudy tragically took his life at their home on North Tatum Boulevard in Phoenix. His sudden death left Joyce devastated and heartbroken. The community mourned his loss, and Rudy was laid to rest in Green Acres Memorial Park in Scottsdale.

Joyce, grappling with her immense grief, found it difficult to move forward. The memory of Rudy and their life together haunted her every moment. Despite the support of her family, Joyce's sorrow grew overwhelming. On July 6, 1977, unable to bear the pain any longer, she went to Rudy's grave at Green Acres, there, at the very spot where her beloved husband rested, Joyce took her own life. She was just 21 years old.

Gutierrez grave marker, 33.454618, -111.907458

The discovery of Joyce's body at Rudy's grave by a caretaker the following morning shocked the community once again. Joyce was laid to rest beside Rudy at Green Acres Memorial Park, a poignant symbol of their undying love and the heartache that defined their final days. Their gravesite stands as a testament to a love story marked by joy, sorrow, and an unbreakable bond that even death could not sever.

Gutierrez gravesite, 2024

The story of Rudy and Joyce Gutierrez serves as a stark reminder of the profound impact of mental health struggles and the importance of support and understanding. Their lives, though short and filled with tragedy, continue to resonate with those who knew them and the community they left behind.

Green Acres Cemetery, established in 1957, has become a quiet hotspot for ghost hunters, many of whom have captured electronic voice phenomena near its mausoleums. Some believe it may be the spirit of Joyce Gutierrez that still drifts through the cemetery, refusing to rest even in death.

Joyce and her husband, Rudy Gutierrez, are buried together in the "Garden of Prayer" section of the Scottsdale cemetery.

Green Acres Cemetery aerial view, 1978

Green Acres Cemetery entrance, 2024

Green Acres Mortuary & Cemetery
401 N. Hayden Rd., Scottsdale, AZ 85257

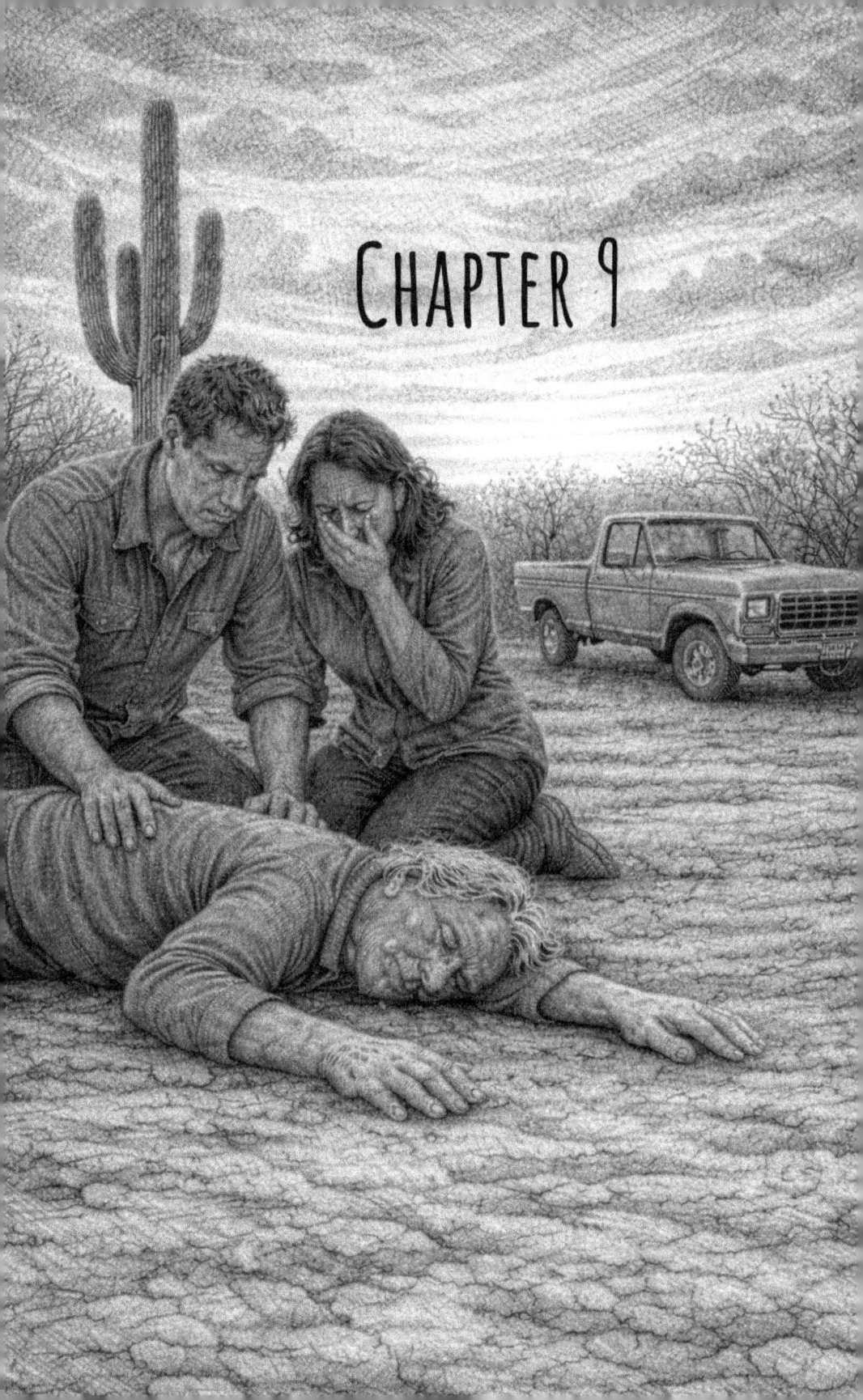

CHAPTER 9

Catherine Maloney, Mesa

Mariposa Gardens, May 20, 1986

Catherine Maloney was born on November 25, 1900, in Babcock, Wisconsin, into a large and close-knit family. Her parents, Frank and Mary Karbowski, instilled in her a strong sense of values and resilience, qualities that would shape her life. In 1928, Catherine married George J. Maloney, and together they raised five children.

After George's death in 1974, Catherine sought solace in the warmer climate of Mesa, where she hoped to enjoy a peaceful retirement. Surrounded by her children and grandchildren, she cherished family gatherings and actively participated in her community, finding joy in the simple pleasures of life.

However, Catherine's life took a tragic and mysterious turn in the spring of 1986. Her body was discovered in a field near what would later become Mariposa Gardens Memorial Park in Mesa. The shocking discovery left her family and the community reeling, as the circumstances surrounding her death remained unclear.

Future location of Mariposa Gardens, 1986

Catherine had gone missing on May 20, but her disappearance wasn't reported until June 12, when her son Emmons returned from vacation and realized she was gone. Despite efforts to find her, it wasn't until 23-year-old construction worker Rudolph Key decided to search the area after hearing about a $5,000 reward that Catherine's body was finally found. Hidden in a small ditch covered with brush, her remains were difficult to spot.

The Maricopa County Sheriff's Office confirmed that there was no foul play involved, as her jewelry and purse were found with her. Investigators believe she may have been walking toward Valley Lutheran Hospital when she collapsed.

Field near Leisure World & Mariposa Gardens, 2024

An autopsy was scheduled to determine the exact cause of death, but the Maricopa County medical examiner had already ruled it as due to natural causes. The tragic end to Catherine's long and full life stands in stark contrast to the rich heritage and love she had built with her family.

Catherine's remains were transported back to Wisconsin, where she was laid to rest in Allouez Catholic Cemetery in Green Bay, beside her beloved husband George. Her grave became a place of mourning and remembrance for her family, who continue to cherish her memory.

Emmons Maloney, while expressing his deep gratitude for the closure, confirmed that the reward money would be paid to Key, the man who brought an end to the uncertainty. "It's a relief to finally know what happened and to be able to lay her to rest," he said.

Catherine Maloney's story is a reminder of life's fragility and the enduring mysteries that sometimes accompany its end. Her life, marked by resilience, love, and family, will be remembered, even as the unanswered questions surrounding her death cast a shadow over her memory.

Mariposa Gardens Memorial Park opened in 1999. Paranormal investigators have reported eerie activity not only within the cemetery but also in nearby Jefferson Park. Shadowy figures have been seen, and some claim a woman in white haunts the area. It's possible that the spirits of those who died at the nearby hospital—including Catherine Maloney—still roam the grounds, unable to find peace.

Leisure World Power Road entrance, 2024

Leisure World & Valley Lutheran Hospital aerial view, 1986

Mariposa Gardens Memorial Park Broadway Road entrance, 2024

Mariposa Gardens Memorial Park
400 S. Power Rd., Mesa, AZ 85206

CHAPTER 10

Jim Chafin, Glendale

Resthaven Park Cemetery, August 8, 1987

Jim Chafin lived a life marked by service and struggle. Born in Kentucky in 1932, he later joined the U.S. Navy, serving during the Korean and Vietnam Wars. By the mid-1980s, Jim moved to Glendale to be closer to his mother, Nellie. He faced numerous challenges during this time, including PTSD and struggles with alcohol. Despite these struggles, he maintained a close relationship with his mom and was known to check on her regularly.

In the middle of the night, on August 8, 1987, a group of young people decided to visit Resthaven Park Cemetery to hunt for ghosts. They stumbled upon a gruesome scene, finding the nude body of a man lying in the northwest corner of the cemetery. Glendale Police later identified the victim as Orison James Chafin Jr.

Resthaven Park Cemetery utility road entrance, 2024

Jim had last been seen the previous day, drinking with friends at a bar near 59th and Glendale Avenues. He left the bar with an unknown male and was never seen alive again. The police investigation revealed that Jim's body bore signs of a violent struggle, with multiple lacerations on his neck and evidence of severe trauma. Several Budweiser bottle caps and cigarette butts were found scattered around the scene, along with broken beer bottles.

Jim Chafin's last known location, formerly Critter's Bar, 2024

Despite a thorough investigation, including interviews with Jim's friends and family, the motive and identity of his killer remained elusive. His mother described him as having a hot temper, often getting into fights when intoxicated. She also mentioned that he had been threatened by a man named "Slim," who had previously expressed violent intentions towards her son.

Jim's case eventually went cold and a flyer issued by the Glendale Police Department called for any information that could help solve the case, but no significant leads emerged. The community was left in shock and sorrow, unable to comprehend the brutal end met by Jim Chafin.

Glendale Police Department cold case flyer

Jim was buried with military honors at the National Memorial Cemetery of Arizona, a testament to his service and sacrifice. His grave stands as a solemn reminder of a life cut short under mysterious and violent circumstances.

National Memorial Cemetery of Arizona, section 25

Jim Chafin's grave marker, 33.696119, -112.018400

Resthaven Park Cemetery was established in 1947 and has been part of the Dignity Memorial national network, one of the largest cemetery conglomerates in the United States, since 1993.

There have been several deaths connected to Resthaven, including a chilling case in 2004 when a teenager was killed during a drug deal gone wrong and buried in one of the graves. Local residents have reported strange experiences—encountering shadowy figures and capturing unexplainable anomalies in photographs. Ghost hunters have also recorded electronic voice phenomena throughout the grounds. Some believe the restless spirit of Jim Chafin still roams the cemetery, searching for his killer.

The unsolved murder of Orison James Chafin Jr. remains a haunting chapter in Glendale's history, a cold case that continues to baffle investigators and tug at the heartstrings of those who knew him. Jim Chafin's grave is located in Section 25 of the National Memorial Cemetery of Arizona in Phoenix.

National Memorial Cemetery of Arizona entrance, 2024

National Memorial Cemetery of Arizona
2929 E. Pinnacle Peak Rd., Phoenix, AZ 85024

Resthaven Park Cemetery aerial view, 2024

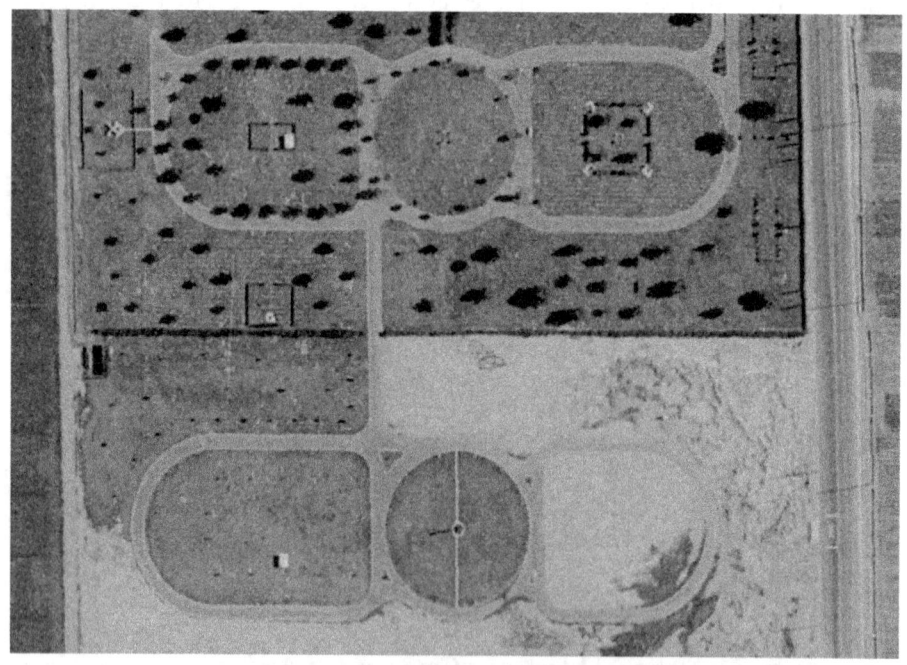

Resthaven Park Cemetery aerial view, 1987

Resthaven Park Cemetery fountain, 2022

Resthaven Park Cemetery
6450 W. Northern Ave., Glendale, AZ 85301

CHAPTER 11

Lee Belshee, Yuma

Sunset Vista Cemetery, August 7, 1997

On a blistering summer afternoon in 1997, tragedy struck at Sunset Vista Cemetery in Yuma. At precisely 2:40 p.m. on August 7, the Yuma County Sheriff's Office received a distress call reporting a potential suicide. Deputy Richey was immediately dispatched to the scene.

Upon his arrival, Deputy Richey found Rural Metro paramedics desperately trying to revive the victim. Despite their efforts, Dr. Haden, the on-call emergency room doctor at Yuma Regional Medical Center, declared the victim dead on arrival. The deceased, identified as Elmer Lee Belshee, was discovered lifeless beside a pickup truck in the cemetery, blood pooling from a self-inflicted gunshot wound to his head, painting a gruesome scene.

A witness, who was en route to the mortuary, reported seeing Lee collapse. He quickly stopped his truck and rushed over, only to discover blood streaming from Lee's head. The witness' account aligned with the observations of paramedic Curt Calaway, who found Lee lying on his right side, a .38 caliber revolver still clutched in his left hand. Calaway carefully removed the weapon, noting that it was fully loaded except for one spent cartridge.

Sunset Vista Cemetery, 2024

As the investigation unfolded, a heartbreaking story emerged. Detective Owens, who arrived shortly after Deputy Richey, discovered that Lee had purchased a funeral plan from Sunset Vista just eleven days earlier, on July 27. A mortuary employee informed Owens that Lee had been suffering from severe medical issues due to a broken neck he had sustained years before.

Inside Lee's wallet, investigators found notes detailing his final wishes and intentions. It became clear that Lee had meticulously planned his departure. Among the items recovered were a memorial guide, an insurance policy dated July 27, 1997, and a letter designating a close friend as the executor of his estate. This letter suggested that Lee had confided in her about his intentions.

When Detective Owens informed the friend of Lee's suicide, she was not surprised. She revealed that Lee had been adamant about not allowing doctors to amputate his legs, a procedure deemed necessary for his condition. This final act was Lee's way of asserting control over his fate.

Sunset Vista Cemetery, veterans section

As the investigation concluded, the tragic reality of Lee Belshee's life and death became evident. A man tormented by physical pain and the impending loss of his independence, he chose to end his life on his own terms. His story, though filled with sorrow, serves as a stark reminder of the profound struggles some people endure, often hidden beneath the surface.

Established in 1985, Sunset Vista Cemetery has become the final resting place for many of Arizona's veterans. After Lee's death on the cemetery grounds, some believe his spirit may still linger—silently walking among the graves of his fallen brothers in arms.

Elmer Lee Belshee, a World War II Navy veteran, was laid to rest alongside his wife Velma in Odd Fellows Cemetery in The Dalles, Oregon.

Sunset Funeral Home, 2024

Sunset Vista Funeral Home, Cemetery, and Crematory, 2024

Sunset Vista Funeral Home, Cemetery, and Crematory
11357 E. 40th St., Yuma, AZ 85367

GLENDALE MEMORIAL PARK

SECURITY

SECURITY

Chapter 12

Barry Brutchey, Glendale

Glendale Memorial Park, December 5, 1998

On a brisk, quiet December night in 1998, the suburban community of Glendale was shocked by the untimely death of Barry Brutchey. Barry, a 44-year-old security guard, was found lifeless in his truck at the entrance of a local cemetery. His supervisor, Kimberly, made the discovery after growing concerned when Barry failed to report his regular "Code-4" status check at 2:00

Glendale Memorial Park, 2024

Barry had been diligently working that night, patrolling Glendale Memorial Park Cemetery to prevent vandalism. At around 1:15 a.m., he had last communicated with his supervisor, assuring her that everything was in order. However, when he didn't check in at the next scheduled time, Kimberly decided to visit the cemetery. Upon arrival, she found Barry slumped against the door of his truck, seemingly asleep.

Kimberly attempted to wake Barry by knocking on the window and shining a flashlight inside the truck. When he didn't respond, she left to call for assistance, adhering to the protocol that supervisors couldn't report guards asleep over the radio. She returned with another security guard and they both tried to rouse Barry, but to no avail. Suspecting something was seriously wrong, they called the Glendale Fire Department.

The paramedics arrived promptly, but it was too late. Barry was pronounced dead at the scene. He was found with his head resting against the window, his boots removed, and several empty cigarette packages scattered around. There were no signs of foul play, leading authorities to conclude it was an unattended death.

Detective Clayton and his partner arrived shortly after to secure the scene and begin their investigation. They contacted Barry's next of kin, eventually reaching his mother in Ohio and his brother in Tempe. It was his brother who came to retrieve Barry's personal belongings and the keys to his truck.

The medical examiner's report later confirmed that Barry had died of natural causes, bringing a somber end to the investigation. This incident, documented in the Glendale Police Department's records, highlights the fragility of life and the importance of the often-overlooked roles individuals like Barry play in our communities. As the night grew colder, Barry's story became another chapter in the annals of Glendale's history, a bitter reminder of the silent heroes who guard our peace and tranquility.

Established in 1895 by Glendale's early settlers, the historic Glendale Memorial Park Cemetery has long been a place of quiet remembrance. Yet over the years, whispers of paranormal activity and eerie encounters have echoed among nearby residents. Following the death of Barry on the grounds, stories of strange happenings seemed to intensify—fueling even more speculation that the cemetery might be haunted.

Barry Brutchey was laid to rest at the Davis Cemetery in Bellaire, Ohio.

Glendale Memorial Park aerial view, 2024

Glendale Memorial Park Cemetery
7844 N. 61st Ave., Glendale, AZ 85301

Chapter 13

Rick Goodspeed, Camp Verde

Clear Creek Cemetery, September 17, 1999

Rick Goodspeed's life was marred by turbulence and tragedy. In May 1991, as the owner of an auto-repair shop in Phoenix, he faced a significant burglary at his business. Overwhelmed by frustration and anger, Rick decided to take drastic measures to protect his property by setting up a booby-trap. He installed a pipe bomb in his shop, intending it to explode like a shrapnel grenade if tampered with.

Fortunately, the Phoenix police discovered the device before it could cause any harm. They called in the bomb squad, which used a sophisticated robot named "SWEE PEA" to safely defuse the bomb. The incident highlighted the dangers of homemade security measures, drawing significant public attention. Rick was arrested and claimed he had been set up by an associate who owed him money.

The arrest marked a significant downturn in Rick's life. A few years later, he suffered another devastating blow with the loss of his wife, Irene, casting a long shadow over his subsequent years. As he grappled with grief, Rick faced ongoing legal troubles and a damaged reputation. To make matters worse, he had a warrant out for his arrest, further complicating his situation.

On September 17, 1999, around noon, a woman visiting Clear Creek Cemetery in Camp Verde to pay respects at a relative's grave noticed a figure lying face up near another gravesite. Initially assuming it was a transient resting, she thought little of it. However, upon closer inspection, she realized the figure was motionless, with blood on his shirt and a gun lying nearby. The woman immediately notified the Camp Verde Marshal's Office.

Detective M. Smith took over the investigation. The body, showing signs of decomposition, was found lying on a marker for Venita Irene Goodspeed, who had passed away in 1995. Further examination confirmed Rick had been in this state for several days.

Clear Creek Cemetery, section O2

Rick was identified through his Arizona driver's license found on him, and he also possessed a Utah driver's license under the name "Bobby Boshers." It was revealed that he had a pending warrant with the U.S. Marshals Office. A search uncovered various personal belongings, including a .45 caliber Colt Revolver and ammunition, indicating that Rick had been prepared for his final act.

A week later, Rick's daughter traveled from Texas to identify her father's body and collect his belongings. Among his personal effects were a mini cassette tape labeled "Jeff," a baseball cap, and an electric hair clipper set.

The final resting place of Rick and his wife became a site of profound tragedy for the Goodspeed family. Haunted by his past and the loss of his beloved wife, Richard chose to end his life at her gravesite. What was once a symbol of love and cherished memories now held a deeper, sorrowful significance.

Richard Goodspeed's story is a stark reminder of how unresolved grief and escalating frustrations can lead to drastic and fatal decisions. His life, marked by significant highs and devastating lows, ultimately ended in a devastating act of finality at the grave of the woman he had lost, bringing a tragic close to his troubled existence.

The earliest burials at Clear Creek Cemetery date back to the 1880s, and the nearby Clear Creek Church was built between 1898 and 1903.

For generations, locals have believed both places to be haunted. On certain nights, a strange mist clings only to the cemetery, vanishing the moment it reaches the gates—an unsettling phenomenon that has fueled ghostly legends. One frequently seen apparition is a teenage girl said to have died by suicide before the cemetery was even established. She drifts from headstone to headstone, as if searching for someone she cannot find. Another chilling tale speaks of two shadowy figures—believed to be failed robbers gunned down during a botched heist, wandering the grounds together in silence. With Rick's passing, there are those who believe he never truly left. Still burdened by sorrow and a love he couldn't let go, some say his spirit now roams Clear Creek Cemetery—just one more lost soul among the many who refuse to rest.

Richard and Irene Goodspeed are buried at Clear Creek Cemetery in Camp Verde. Richard was interred in the Jones family plot, alongside his wife, in Section O2.

Goodspeed grave marker, 34.525806, -111.827654

Clear Creek Cemetery, 2024

Clear Creek Cemetery
2939 S. Old Church Rd., Camp Verde, AZ 86322

Afterword

As we reach the end of our journey through *Haunted Arizona Deadly Graveyards*, I want to extend my heartfelt thanks to you, the reader, for exploring these shadowy and storied corners of Arizona with me. This book is more than a mere catalog of haunted locations; it's a tribute to the lives once lived, the mysteries that linger, and the respect that must always be given.

Should you decide to venture out and visit any of the cemeteries featured within these pages, I urge you to approach these sacred spaces with the utmost reverence and consideration. Cemeteries are places of profound significance, where the echoes of the past meet the quiet of the present. Many visitors come to honor their loved ones, while others seek to connect with the spirits that may remain. Whether you are a curious explorer or a seeker of the supernatural, remember that compassion is key.

Be mindful of the grieving families who may be paying their respects during your visit. Their moments of sorrow and reflection are sacred, and your presence should always be respectful and unobtrusive. Additionally, if you choose to attempt communication with any spirits, it is both courteous and prudent to clearly say goodbye, ensuring that any lingering energies do not follow you away from the site.

Many of the cemeteries discussed in this book are located on private property. Therefore, please adhere to the designated visiting hours and any other guidelines set forth by the property owners. This ensures that these historical and hallowed grounds are preserved and respected for future generations.

Acknowledgments

Acknowledgments

I want to extend my deepest gratitude to the spirits whose stories have filled these pages. Though your lives ended in tragedy within these haunted graveyards, your lingering presence and the echoes of your pasts have become the foundation for this book. It is through your experiences that I have been able to delve into the mysteries and histories that make Arizona's cemeteries both eerie and fascinating.

Each one of you has left a lasting impression on these sacred grounds, and it is my hope that by sharing your stories, I honor your memories and shed light on the lives you once lived. Your stories have not only enriched this book but also deepened my understanding of the thin veil between the living and the dead.

Thank you for allowing me to be a part of your stories and for guiding me through the shadows. This book is as much yours as it is mine, and I am grateful for the opportunity to tell your tales.

Dedication

This book is dedicated to my family. Without you, it would never have come to life. Thank you for putting up with me through the writing process and for your endless support. You are truly amazing, and I love you all dearly!

To my wonderful woman, your patience and love have been my anchor. To my kids – my big boy, thanks for bringing me all those bottles of pop when I needed them while pounding away on the keyboard. My little girl, thank you for sneaking me snacks that Mommy said I shouldn't have and for hanging out, watching and re-watching old episodes of *Twilight Zone* and *Are You Afraid of the Dark* with me. And to my teenage son, thank you for helping me get acclimated to the Arizona heat so I could get out and take the photos for the book. You are all my greatest source of inspiration and joy. To my adult daughter, I hope one day we can bridge the gap between us. And to ~~the one-eyed feline pest,~~ Jinxycat, for licking my face nightly and waking me up, reminding me to stay up late for just a few more hours, to work some more on the book.

A special thanks to my grueling summer job at the meat supplier, driving a semi-truck in over 115° heat with no air conditioner through the desert. Your misery funded this book, and for that, I am strangely grateful. Shout-out to my acupuncturist, thank you for alleviating the pain from the summer job and endless hours of writing. I appreciate you taking care of the aches and pains that my wife kindly avoided.

Lastly, to those of you still holding and reading books, thank you! While the stories within these pages might already be floating around the internet, you chose to support my work by buying this book. Your support enables me to continue researching and sharing these tales. Thank you for being a part of this journey.

Bibliography

Bibliography

Chapter 1: John Moore, Phoenix
"Aged Pioneer Of State Since 1867, Despondent, Commits Suicide On Grave Of Wife," *Arizona Republic* (Phoenix, AZ) 26 Apr 1924
"John W. Moore" memorial, *Find A Grave*, https://www.findagrave.com/memorial/217026955
"Rebeca Drumm Moore" memorial, *Find A Grave*, https://www.findagrave.com/memorial/217648095

Chapter 2: James Mitchell, Phoenix
"Kills Self At Wife's Grave In Cemetery Here," *Arizona Republic* (Phoenix, AZ) 17 Aug 1926
"James Mitchell" memorial, *Find A Grave*, https://www.findagrave.com/memorial/159598405
"Mrs. James Tartin Mitchell" memorial, *Find A Grave*, https://www.findagrave.com/memorial/159355546

Chapter 3: Eulogio Molina, Nogales
Aerial Photo, *USGS* (1975-05-27 - 1975-05-30)
"Aged Gravedigger Dies in Cemetery," *Arizona Daily Star* (Tucson, AZ) 9 Jun 1930
"Eulogio Molina" memorial, *Find A Grave*, https://www.findagrave.com/memorial/267754164

Chapter 4: Julian Holmes, Phoenix
Aerial Photo, *Landiscor* (1955-12-10 - 1955-12-11)
"Grieving Man Ends Life On Wife's Grave," *Arizona Republic* (Phoenix, AZ) 24 Feb 1954
"William Edwin Julian Holmes Sr." memorial, *Find A Grave*, https://www.findagrave.com/memorial/6188617
"Margaret Sanders Holmes" memorial, *Find A Grave*, https://www.findagrave.com/memorial/6188781

Bibliography

Chapter 5: Andres Serna, Superior
Aerial Photo, *USGS* (1945-11-06 - 1945-11-08)
"Dog Keeps Vigil After Owner Dies," *Tucson Citizen* (Tucson, AZ) 20 Jun 1956
"Andres Serna" memorial, *Find A Grave*, https://www.findagrave.com/memorial/171345347

Chapter 6: Rob Gastelum, Tucson
Aerial Photo, *USDA* (1958-01-20 - 1958-02-17)
"Veteran 24, Succumbs Of Self-Inflicted Wound," *Arizona Daily Star* (Tucson, AZ) 8 Feb 1957
"Robert S. Gastelum" obituary, *Arizona Daily Star* (Tucson, AZ) 10 Feb 1957
"Robert Smith Gastelum" memorial, *Find A Grave*, https://www.findagrave.com/memorial/146132143

Chapter 7: Ward Bradish, Tucson
Aerial Photo, *USDA* (1967-04-10 - 1967-05-12)
"Body Found In Cemetery Identified," *Tucson Daily Citizen* (Tucson, AZ) 11 Nov 1964
"Ward Orin Bradish Sr." memorial, *Find A Grave*, https://www.findagrave.com/memorial/29309641

Chapter 8: Joyce Gutierrez, Scottsdale
Aerial Photo, *LandisCor* (1978-12-14 - 1978-12-31)
"Rudolph Gutierrez" obituary, *Arizona Republic* (Phoenix, AZ) 12 Dec 1975
"Widow found dead at husband's grave," *Arizona Republic* (Phoenix, AZ) 7 Jul 1977
"Joyce Marian Boudette Gutierrez" memorial, *Find A Grave*, https://www.findagrave.com/memorial/223282975
"Rudolph V. 'Rudy' Gutierrez" memorial, *Find A Grave*, https://www.findagrave.com/memorial/215417511

Chapter 9: Catherine Maloney, Mesa
Aerial Photo, *LandisCor* (1986-05-25 - 1986-06-14)
"Missing woman's body found in field; Mesa man may get $5000 reward," *Arizona Republic* (Phoenix, AZ) 16 Jul 1986
"Mesa woman died of natural causes, coroner rules," *Arizona Republic* (Phoenix, AZ) 17 Jul 1986
"Mrs. George (Catherine) Maloney" obituary, *Green Bay Press-Gazette* (Green Bay, WI) 17 Jul 1986
"Catherine Karbowski Maloney" memorial, *Find A Grave*, https://www.findagrave.com/memorial/123049010

Chapter 10: Jim Chafin, Glendale
Aerial Photo, *LandisCor* (1987-11-20 - 1987-11-20)
Glendale Police Department Report No. I87043644
Glendale Police Department, https://www.glendaleaz.com/live/city_services/public_safety/police_department/reporting/homicide_cold_case_information
"Slaying victim is found in cemetery," *Arizona Republic* (Phoenix, AZ) 9 Aug 1987
"Body dumped in cemetery identified," *Arizona Republic* (Phoenix, AZ) 10 Aug 1987
"Orison J. Chafin Jr." obituary, *Arizona Republic* (Phoenix, AZ) 12 Aug 1987 "Orison Chafin Jr." memorial, *Find A Grave*, https://www.findagrave.com/memorial/480630

Chapter 11: Lee Belshee, Yuma
Yuma County Sheriff's Department Case No. 97-13285
"Elmer Lee Belshee" memorial, *Find A Grave*, https://www.findagrave.com/memorial/112768390

Chapter 12: Barry Brutchey, Glendale
Glendale Police Department Report No. I98122539
"Barry Gene Brutchey" memorial, *Find A Grave*,
https://www.findagrave.com/memorial/225889446

Chapter 13: Rick Goodspeed, Camp Verde
Camp Verde Marshal Office Report No. V99005106
"SWEE PEA tackles explosive tasks," *Arizona Republic* (Phoenix, AZ)
10 May 1991
"Booby trap defused in shop," *Arizona Republic* (Phoenix, AZ) 10 May
1991   "Richard M. Goodspeed III" memorial, *Find A Grave*,
https://www.findagrave.com/memorial/19210748
"V. Irene Goodspeed" memorial, *Find A Grave*,
https://www.findagrave.com/memorial/19210734

www.ingramcontent.com/pod-product-compliance
Lightning Source LLC
Chambersburg PA
CBHW061659120626
46550CB00003B/1015